For Kim, Rich, Tim and Robbie.

www.fast-print.net/store.php

ME AND MY LAMP
Copyright © Howard G Awbery 2014

A catalogue record for this book is available from the
British Library

ISBN 978-178456-152-9

First published 2014 by FASTPRINT PUBLISHING of
Peterborough, England.

Contents

Why Choose Mining?

My name is Howard G Awbery and at the time of writing this, the year is 2014 I am 68 years old and feel 34. My daughter, Kim suggested that, 'before it's too late,' (which is a euphemism for, just in case I die soon) I should put pen to paper and write down some of the stories from my career in the British coal mining industry. To me they weren't stories; it was just as it was, but to my wide-eyed children the stories came from an incomprehensible world, full of delightful characters who were real, fascinating and full of fun. To the generations of Awberys I trust will follow, hopefully these chapters will be an insight into a world where I was one of the last coal miners who 'filled' my 'stint' of coal, i.e. loaded coal with a shovel that was so big it was called an elephant's tab (ear), shouted 'FI...RE' when I used explosives and, worked in the shaft, on 8" girders with a 600 yard drop beneath my feet.

The years sometimes dim the recall but in my case the opposite is true. My memories of that wonderful industry are vivid. I will try to be disciplined and not embellish the stories nor invent colours that were never there. My endeavour will be to describe the incidents to the best of my memory, for in the main they need no embellishment and can standalone. However, I promise the reader that if poetic licence is used, it will be used sparingly.

My certificate says I worked in the coal industry for 29 years and 10 months but let's call it a round 30 years.

My career was not a jail sentence as some of my friends who worked in Local Authorities describe their careers; denigrating every day they worked or did their 'stretch', waiting for their pensions. My career was a colourful 30 years of fun, tragedy, tears and good humour.

I started working in 1964 for what was in those days called The National Coal Board and finished working in 1994 for what became fashionably called, British Coal. I worked in South Wales, Nottinghamshire and Buckinghamshire. Buckinghamshire I hear you ask; the coal industry? Yes, I worked at The Vache for two years, the industry's management development centre. The Vache was nestled in the 'heart of the coal mining industry' (I jest), 20 miles from London. A stately home set in 50 acres of Buckinghamshire countryside, sporting its own lake complete with swans and not a cobble of coal to be seen for 100 miles in any direction and never likely to be.

Remember, these were the good old days when British Coal's London HQ, Hobart House looked over into Buckingham Palace gardens, when Colliery Managers were kings and Area Directors were gods. 20 miles from London was quite convenient for the coal politicians and British Coal's HQ staff to secrete themselves away for a night or two.

When I started work in 1964 there were 534 collieries operating and 491,000 employees working in the Industry. Thirty years later there were only 16 collieries left, populated by just 7,400 employees, such was the systematic rape of the industry. The systematic rape of our great nation's energy reserves by the inept and myopic politicians of the day; politicians completely incapable of producing a cohesive UK energy strategy for an island mounted on coal, buffeted by strong winds, surrounded by gas and graced by clockwork dependable tides.

But the statistic that has stuck in my mind until today is that we killed a man a day. The British coal mining industry killed a man a day! 365 - one for every day of the week including Saturdays and Sundays, Christmas Day and New Year's Day, year in year out. This was a salutary statistic for someone about to join an industry that had never, to my knowledge, previously employed an Awbery.

This lack of mining heritage was challenged when I was asked at my interview to join the South Wales coal mining industry, 'Now Howard, have you any family who currently work or have recently worked in the coal mining industry.' I answered, 'yes certainly Sir,' just to impress, 'I understand I had a great uncle Willy who once worked down the pit for a week, but he broke his leg on the face and left to become a farmer. I never actually met him as I think it all happened in the 1920s.' The interviewing panel laughed.

It is more than likely that, with four sets of working class grandparents from South Wales, some Awberys or Thomases or Roberts or Jenkins worked at some time in the South Wales coal mining industry.

In 1964 my mother and father moved from London back to Swansea, my father's original home and I followed shortly after. A few applications later to local large organisations and I was successful in being offered three student apprenticeships in South Wales; one with the Steel Company of Wales, one with the Welsh equivalent of the Electricity Board and one with the National Coal Board. Getting through interviews with a golden tongue, inherited from my MP grandfather on my father's side was easy; studying and passing exams was always the difficult bit for me for there were always more interesting things to do.
I considered each of the options in turn to determine my future.

One weekend I drove to The Steel Company of Wales, and what I saw led me to believe it already had been closed down. What was left was spread out along seven miles of the South Wales coastline; seven miles of dereliction and scrap. As I travelled alongside The Steel Company of Wales on the M4 the site appeared to me to be a shambles of industrial buildings and fiery chimneys as if emptied from a child's toy box and then randomly arranged. How could it be 'OK' to leave such a disgraceful heritage? My father explained that the whole steel industry had been on the brink of complete abandonment before the politicians woke up to the consequences of its imminent demise.

Just seconds before a recovery was too late in economic terms, the guilty politicians appeased the electorate and invested again in The Steel Company of Wales. The weary industry, in its death-throws, spluttered and coughed slowly back into life. It grew again, leaving in its wake, miles of dead and dying buildings never cleared to this day. As I drove along the M4 corridor all I saw was a myriad of pipes, flames and smoke under a sulphurous yellow sky in the worst place man had created in South Wales. The place was called Port Talbot. I cringed at the thought of arriving every day to work in The Steel Company of Wales.

Turning my attention to the South Wales Electricity Board, I never understood electricity at college and hated impedance, conductivity, amps, volts drops and anything else that couldn't be touched... more than once. If I hadn't understood electricity at college and wasn't immediately inspired to learn more as I surveyed the impressive spider's web of the National Grid, covering the whole of Wales with a massive 33,000 volts humming through its veins, then I needed to fight shy of such a career.

But coal mining, now that was different. Quite apart from the conceptual leaps in technical achievement from the old hand-filling days, coal mining was responsible for a social heritage going back hundreds of years. Coal mining had been the very foundation upon which South Wales' industries had been built and in its wake, the necessary and colourful Socialist movement had been born.

My sleepy Welsh ancestry was provoking a strange curiosity in me at the thought of working down the pit.

I felt I was being encouraged to find out more about this evocative industry. Encouragements were being fired at me from all sides by past generations of Welsh, Awbery colliers, long since forgotten. I felt there to be a gentle persuasion taking place, a nudging towards coal by the combined forces of Providence and my Welsh ancestors.

Providence, for there was opportunity in coal mining and my ancestors who were willing me to experience their values and simple way of life. They were keen for me to understand what was really important in life, to ground my young, airy-fairy views; to help me understand the meaning and richness of true camaraderie and trust and dependency on others in one of the few environments where men still lived by these values.

I didn't recognise the gentle pushes I was experiencing at the time. Why coal mining, why me? I'd been brought up in London so why was I becoming so stirred by the idea of working down the pit? Excitement and fear were driving me. Why had I become so moved by a colliery male voice choir to feel tears welling up inside me as they sang about the industry? What was drawing me towards this underground world?

I believe now that my path was gently signposted by my ancestors and when Providence added her weight the decision was made for me. A decision to experience a life where the absence of sunshine, fresh air, green fields and sky gave them such a special pure value, understood only by coal miners. Somewhere in my genes there must have been coal dust and before it was too late and the politicians destroyed the British coal mining industry as they had done to the British steel industry, the British fishing industry and the British shipbuilding industry, the gods and my ancestors were plotting to ensure that another Awbery would be privileged to savour the experience of working underground and see, at first hand, Mother Nature's treasure chest.

To me at 19 the very thought of working in a pit was a testosterone-igniting challenge that made my very soul tremble. Real men worked down the pit; down the pit there was danger; down the pit there was the unknown. Down the pit I would be working with men who had a code that superseded all other codes, down the pit men I would be working with men who lived in the real now.

And so I chose coal mining and my ancestors were oh, so, so right.

I also learned the importance of living in the real now.

Chapter 1 - My Very First Day

Slowly we slid beneath the surface of Wales. A few more carefully measured, vertical yards and then the bottom of the cage fell from beneath my boots. 11 men and me, in absolute darkness dropped silently towards the centre of the earth. And then there was blackness, an all-consuming blackness that can be felt but can't be touched…

The 12 of us rocketed towards a secret world of work that had survived, in some form or other, for over a thousand years. An underground microcosm of work that those who have never ventured below ground can only imagine and their imaginations makes them shudder within. To those who have never ventured below ground the very concept of working by candlelight, in a confined space, breathing black dust is the fuel of nightmares.

The 12 of us flew towards a world of activity where the value of, 'black stone that burns' had already been realised many years before; coal… the currency of power. Ever since the black stone had been found it had been exploited. More coal, more heat, more heat, more power, more power, more industry, more industry, the ultimate… more money.

We were packed into a steel box suspended on a single thread of steel rope, little more than an inch diameter. 12 men invading each other's space, sharing the smells of yesterday's locker-dried sweaty clothes, last night's beer, 'just a couple of pints' and the unmistakable stale smell of the recent last cigarette.

Most colliers smoked and there were smoking rituals to be observed before going underground. The last cigarette before the shift began would have been one of just two, loose cigarettes and two, loose matches carefully carried on top of every man's food tin. Totally naked apart from a pair of flip flops made from old conveyor belting and carrying only a towel, the two cigarettes and matches were transported, like treasure, from the clean side of the baths to the dirty side. Once in the dirty side, steel toe-capped boots curled like Aladdin's shoes in the hot lockers, stiff trousers, sweat dried shirts, helmet, working jacket and knee pads were donned and then the journey continued on to the lamp room to start the shift, still carrying the two treasured cigarettes and two matches.

In the lamp room the heavy cap lamp battery would be slid onto the thick leather belt along with a self-rescuer and the long cap lamp cable hung around the neck; the cap lamp was never attached to the helmet at this time. Brightly polished flame lamps were collected here by officials and those men who would be working alone for long periods.

At this point, one cigarette and one match would be secreted in a small, dry hole in the brickwork of the lamp room or balanced upon a ledge, out of sight, ready and waiting for the owner to return emerging from the cage at the end of his shift.

When the owner did return, blinded by the white light of day at the end of the shift, but coal dust black as the ace of spades, the precious cache would be raided by its yearning owner. Across a red, phosphorous marked, rough stone wall the match would be drawn following its familiar moon shape journey and the freshly lit cigarette smoked in deep, long, savoured draughts. The smoke would be exhaled slowly and blown upwards through pursed lips. The cigarette would be smoked as if it restored new life into its recipient, in comparison with the dust-laden underground air this was heaven; such was the irony of the moment. Remember, before you judge these colliers they often worked on their knees in only three feet of height or less for a full shift. To them there was little thought of the future. 'Now' was their only future and they looked forward to, and relished their first cigarette. They savoured the moment as only smokers can.

On the 6.00 am walk from the lamp room to the cage, before the shift started, the first cigarette would have been equally ritually smoked. The pace of the walk to the shaft-side would be measured, as it had been a thousand times before to arrive with only the cigarette butt left. Flicking the smoking butt away the smoker would watch the red tip arc upwards and then explode as it hit the ground exactly one second before he entered the covered area of the pit top. This pre-shift smoking ritual always reminded me of, 'any last requests' and the post-shift ritual as, 'a prayer of thanksgiving'.

Secreting cigarettes and matches about one's person to take them down the pit to smoke in secret was such a taboo act that smoking materials were referred to as contraband and searches carried out on every man on every shift. The risks to men who worked below ground of someone inadvertently igniting gas by smoking were huge and every miner knew them. Too many natural phenomena capable of causing explosions were faced daily, to introduce an unnecessary, man-made, risk was criminal.

Contraband contravention was rare, dismissal automatic and offenders were ostracised by the other miners and their families; such were the risks of illegally smoking underground.

Squashed in the tiny cage the smell of stale, second-hand cigarette smoke lingered on men's breath; in this close proximity it was inescapable.

The cage floor resumed its place beneath our boots as the winder man on the surface gently started to apply the brakes. The lights of the approaching pit bottom dimly lit the shaft walls as we approached. Descending slower by the foot and brighter by the yard the cage slowly entered the pit bottom. The only sound that could be heard was of the four corner guide ropes that steadied the cage, way above in the shaft, jangling, occasionally 'kissing' the shaft walls. The cage with its payload of young men floated gently into the pit bottom.

On the surface the winder man, who controlled the cage's descent, watched as the chalk mark on the drum of steel rope lined up with a similar chalk mark on the huge brake and brought the cage to rest as lightly as a wren landing on a twig.

Day one of thirty years of working in the British coal mining industry had just begun. Little did I know that in the next thirty years working underground I would be involved in underground fires, gas outbursts, being buried under a fall, fatalities, a ghost, major falls of ground, colliery celebrations and three national strikes and it was all to start this very day.

***

My first working day started normally enough, what am I talking about, normally enough! 5.00 am, wasn't normal, not for an 18 year old, 9.00am was normal, maybe 10.00am, but not 5.00 am, 5.00 am was still yesterday!!! My two-bell, Smiths Early Bird alarm clock danced on the windowsill deliberately out of reach from my bed. It seemed I had only just fallen asleep. The fears of my first day at work in the pit were brazened out to my family but secretly my mind hadn't been settled and I had tossed and turned till the early hours.

I can now admit how apprehensive I had been the night before whilst watching my mother prepare my food. To this day I can remember exactly what I had; chicken sandwiches on brown bread with real butter, a Jaffa orange and a flask of coffee, a veritable feast.

I had to remove the Penguin biscuit as it was covered in silver paper. (Silver paper was seen as contraband as it had the property of creating a spark hot enough to ignite gas when struck by a stone or similar heavy object). A few days on I mentioned to my mother I was partial to cheese in my sandwiches, so every day I had cheese; every working day from that day on I got cheese. Caerphilly, Cheddar, Edam, the type of cheese changed, but always cheese. The orange was abandoned when I suggested it was difficult to peel and eat an orange underground. Then there was a sudden realisation by my mother. A real light bulb moment followed by the question:

"Well, surely you wash your hands before you eat your food?"

Peals of laughter came from my father who had worked at Barry Docks when he was young.

The flask broke on its first outing as I rode illegally out of the mine on a conveyor belt following my supervisor. Cheese sandwiches, an apple and a bottle of water were my working companions from that day on.

I never told my mother I had to tie my food up with a used piece of detonator wire and hang it off the roof bars so the mice couldn't get at it. Sometimes when you found yourself working away from your food and it was pitch black you would spin around and your cap lamp beam would catch sight of a gymnastic mouse swinging perilously around and around. The mouse was climbing down the thin wire by its tiny claws on its way to bore a hole straight through my cheese sandwiches. Taking one sandwich and scurrying away wouldn't have been so bad, but they had a habit of munching a hole straight through all of the sandwiches. A lump of rock usually discouraged the miscreant. My mother would have died had she known, bless her.

I'm sure her mind was far away remembering the days when, as a little girl she watched her mother, that is my grandmother, who lived with us until she was 102 years old, prepare food for her husband. My grandfather was a coal trimmer. Coal trimmers went into the holds of coal ships at Barry Docks with huge shovels. Their job was to ensure the cargo of fine coal was levelled for the ship's stability at sea. If you thought coal mining was tough then you should try coal trimming. Coal had claimed her father, who with his lungs full of coal dust, had to sit up in bed to breathe with windows wide open, even on the coldest of nights and here she was making food for her son to wrestle his living out of the same, unforgiving black 'stone that burns'. I should have been more thoughtful.

My father woke me with the sound of the alarm still ringing in the room. Switching it off I remember exactly what he said to this day: "This is the first day of your working life, Howie. I've woken you to make sure you're not late for work on your very first day. Tomorrow you are on your own!" He shared with me some years later that these had been the very same words his father had woken him with on his very first working day. He had never been late for work in thirty years and neither was I.

Soon after a solitary breakfast I was heading for the pit some 15 miles away. My transport was a Triumph 21 motorbike, a 350 cc twin that had served me well. I remember the day was clear and the weather good it being August.

When my mother and father returned to live by the sea in Swansea from London they bought a house in Sketty. Sketty was considered a smart part of Swansea where the 'crachach' (posh folk) lived and according to the men I worked with posh Sketty folk had their coal delivered in 'sex'. I'd been to the pit a few times to get my bearings and the journey was easy. I arrived at 5.40 am at Morlais Colliery on my very first day.

Now, Morlais Colliery had been sunk way back in 1883 and was 150 yards deep. The colliery was serviced by a drift and a shaft, the shaft being only 12 feet in diameter. In its heyday Morlais Colliery had employed 600 men and produced 60,000 tons of coal in a year by working the 6ft and the 4ft seams by hand. Morlais Colliery's claim to fame was that it was the last steam wound cage in South Wales operated by its original winder; a fact I found disconcerting in 1964.

I was introduced to my supervisor Ray Jenkins and escorted through the pit head baths, first the clean side to strip off and naked as the day I was born, carry just my towel and food and walk to the dirty side of the baths to get dressed into my working clothes. On this my first day I was to start with clean clothes, but from then on I would be, along with everyone else, dressing in yesterday's dirty work clothes. On to the lamp room where I was issued with a cap lamp, a self-rescuer and some brass checks. The round check was to be handed in at the shaft side when going down the pit and the square check to be handed in when I returned to the surface. This was a simple check on the number of men underground at any one time. In the event of a serious fire or explosion they were also a means of identification. Ray Jenkins and I travelled to the shaft side together. The descent into the pit was as I described earlier.

Underground we walked the one and a half miles to our place of work. Early on in my career I found distances underground baffling, also directions.

There seemed to be huge distances to be travelled to get to where we worked. However, if you remember that the pit had been turning coal for about 60 years before I was even born, it didn't seem so far, but for a long time it was a feature I struggled to comprehend.

Another concept baffling to the underground newcomer were the terms, 'inbye and outbye'. Inbye was anywhere between you and the furthest reaches of the pit and outbye was anywhere between you and the shafts. Obvious, isn't it?

The roadways we travelled were about 12ft wide x 9ft high. On one side of the roadway a 3ft wide conveyor belt ran on rollers in a steel frame that, in turn, was suspended from the steel arches which supported the roof. The conveyor was running in the opposite direction to the way we travelled inbye to work. The conveyor transported the coal outbye towards the pit bottom.

Beneath my feet was a set of rails with sleepers set at the most inconvenient spacing imaginable. My step seemed always to be too long or too short between the sleepers. How the ponies managed with four hooves was beyond me. I stumbled along behind my supervisor and his byti (workmate). Their gait was even and continuous, randomly spaced sleeper holes or not. My gait was ungainly, clumsy and noisy. The skill of walking whilst watching the roof and also watching the uneven floor was something I was soon to master or suffer the skinned shins and consequential bruising of arms and shoulders. Walking into a low board whilst your eyes were fixed on where to plant your feet was something you only did once. Even with your helmet on it jarred every vertebrae and sat you on your rear end shuddering like a piano tuning fork for several minutes.

Excavated in the floor, on the opposite side of the roadway to the conveyor belt, was a gully along which tumbled an evil torrent of ochre water. The gullies needed permanent maintenance to ensure the huge quantity of water flowing reached the far off sumps; otherwise this amount of water would soon flood the whole pit or part thereof.

Along the roadway, great white and green fungus gardens adorned every piece of timber where the clear water from the roof made its way down the pit props and lagging boards to join the ochre torrent below. The humid temperature and the minerals from the water became a feast for the slow growing fungi. The smell of damp living fungi and mine air is a smell that I will never forget.

Another concept that intrigued me was the phenomena of floor lift. Now, I could understand that the whole of Glamorganshire sits on millions and millions of tons of rock and its weight pressing down on the flimsy steel or wooden roadway supports, even though they are set only a yard apart, would distort them. I could understand that some of this weight would squeeze in the sides of these roadway supports but what came as a shock was the amount of, what was called, floor lift.

Floor lift is where the floor literally fills the roadway over time by pressure from below. In Morlais Colliery, which was a Welsh speaking pit, the term was 'pookins' and teams of men were constantly at work chopping out the pookins and restoring the roadways to their original height. If not continuously maintained the roadways became unusable in a matter of months. So it wasn't just about filling coal, there were all these ancillary tasks to be carried out even before a cobble of coal could be filled.

Half an hour of me ducking and diving and we arrived at 2C's heading. Working after such a journey seemed impossible. I felt I had already completed a full shift. We each took off our jackets and had a well-earned drink from lukewarm water bottles. 2Cs heading was a 12ftx9ft' roadway being driven to open a new area of coal. The coal seam was about 4ft thick and of good quality.

The roadway had to be driven as cheaply as possible. This meant sending out to the surface as little of the stone that overlay the coal as possible. To drive a roadway 9ft high where the coal is only 4 ft thick meant that 5ft of stone had to be disposed of. This was achieved by excavating the coal for an extra 9ft both sides of the 12ft roadway. This resultant void at the sides of the roadway was supported on timber props and then packed with the stone generated when the top was fired down to make the roadway 9 ft high.

Two shifts worked this sequence and we moved forward at a snail's pace of about four yards a week. My impatience for faster rates of roadway advancement never left me in 30 years. By the end of my career 100 metres of drivage in a roadway that was 12ft high by 14ft wide in a week, using state-of-the-art machinery was commonplace throughout the industry.

For six months I worked 2C's heading under supervision, boring the holes to fire the explosives, helping to prepare the stemming and rounds of explosives for the stone ripping and the coal, filling the coal off by hand, setting props and bars and finally setting permanent steel roadway supports.

I was taught to tap the roof with my mandrel (a thin bladed pick) to listen for the dull sound that dared me to challenge its unreliable adherence. I was taught to listen for the roof that sounded like a bell when tapped, which meant it was safe. On one occasion during the first few weeks of working on 2c's heading I remember my supervisor's byti known as Iefan George suggesting gently I come out from the place I was working for a few minutes. I watched in amazement as the roof collapsed over the very spot where I had been just a few minutes earlier. I remember asking him, 'How long before I will be able to predict a fall like you,' and his smiled reply was. 'Soon, soon... about 20 years soon'.

I rode out illegally on the conveyor belt behind my supervisor on my first day and watched, as I lay flat out on the lumpy coal, the roadway supports flash by at what seemed to be 100 mph. I saw the spears of broken timbers above my head and couldn't wait to be through them. Getting off the fast moving, low conveyor was a gymnastic feat, especially after my first day's work, as every part of my body ached like toothache.

After the ride and shortened return walk we eventually arrived at the shaft side and waited for the cage. I stood alongside all the other men on my shift and I was the same colour. To the casual observer I was a collier. However, it wasn't until 30 years later I felt comfortable calling myself a collier.

Chapter 2 - The Day Glamorgan Moved

The verruca had to be cut out. 'And how long would I need to be off work?' I inquired.

'About two weeks,' was the doctor's reply.

I had been working at Brynlliw Colliery near Swansea for 11 weeks out of a period of 12 weeks necessary to complete my face training. The colliery, like so many in this area, had a chequered history.

Brynlliw Colliery was a tough place to work and many accidents happened on the face where I was being trained. I was home early, on average, one day a week, having carried out a colleague on a stretcher or accompanied one who had been injured or what was colloquially referred to as 'having been trapped'. I was dispensable, only being a trainee and I was always happy to volunteer and be home early.

If you have ever watched a war film where two medics rush on to the battlefield, roll an injured man onto a stretcher and run off to safety with him I can assure you it doesn't work like that in practice. To carry an injured man a mile underground takes about eight men; eight men continually stopping, lowering the stretcher, changing hands, left hand first then changing over to the right hand, front of the stretcher then the middle then the back. This was never truer when travelling over rough ground, squeezing the stretcher through narrow spaces and stooping through low height. So I became an adept stretcher-bearer.

The face that I worked on, S7, was a real social experiment. It was a face completely made up of miners from the North-East of England. The whole face team had moved with their families from a colliery near Newcastle and now lived in the same street of caravans awaiting their new houses to be built near Brynlliw Colliery; the fitter, the electrician, the Deputy, the face men, the rippers and even the switchman. It was strange to hear a full face of miners all speaking with Geordie accents in a Welsh-speaking pit. Welsh is a difficult language to master but Geordie is almost impossible!

Brynlliw Colliery had been sunk in 1903 to a depth of 340ft to access the rich anthracite seams. During the coal depression it ceased production in 1925 but reopened again in 1960 working the 6ft and the 3ft seams. In colliery folk law on S2's face on 17 May 1963, five men were buried under a fall, four of them fatally. The fifth man, the under manager, survived by building a wall around himself under the fall until he was rescued. They really were hard men. In 1975 Brynlliw produced 200,000 tons of coal by 570 men. The colliery closed in 1983.

The verruca referred to earlier, was duly cut out and after two weeks convalescence I was given the option to stay on for a further week at Brynlliw Colliery, or dispense with the last week and go on to my next phase of training. I decided to return to complete my 12 weeks of face training. A bad mistake!

My 'stint' of 35 yards of hand-operated props and steel link bars was situated on S7's 200-yard plough face near the centre of the face where the coal was particularly hard. My job was to wait until the triangular plough with its hardened teeth had ripped out six inches of coal the length of the face. Its special shape guided the cut coal onto the steel conveyor called a Panzer conveyor. Each time the plough went through my stint I advanced the Panzer conveyor by six inches using hydraulic rams. When the plough had travelled the length of the face five times and the Panzer conveyor had been advanced 30 inches, my job then was to unset the hand set props that were furthest back from the face and move them forward to support the newly exposed roof over the Panzer conveyor. The exposed roof behind the face now no longer supported by props crashed to the floor.

Unfortunately, the coal in my 'stint' was so hard that the rest of the seam above the cut coal didn't break off as it should and of the 10ft high seam in my stint, 7ft was left hanging onto the roof. Before I could move the supports forward over the Panzer conveyor I needed to break down the over-hanging coal. The only way to get the coal down was to stand on the Panzer conveyor spill pan whilst it was still running and, using a hand held pneumatic jigger pick similar to the ones they use on the roads, jigger the hanging coal down onto the Panzer conveyor. I stepped onto the spill plate as I had done a dozen times before and lifting the jigger pick to my shoulder, started to break the top coal down, bit by bit.

Holding a jigger pick at this height, including the air supply pipe, is no mean feat and the tiredness in your arms made your muscles scream after only a few minutes. The noise was deafening, being that close to your ear, and the vibrations would stay within your hands and fingertips for hours. Progress was slow and as the coal broke off and fell onto the continuously moving Panzer conveyor, it was an effort to retain your balance. After half an hour of continuously jiggering and balancing I was, to coin a phrase, jiggered. Just one more minute using the deafening pick and I would see a large piece of coal drop with the satisfaction that I wouldn't have to stop the face and get help to keep up with the other colliers.

It fell onto the Panzer conveyor with a huge crash, a piece as big as a small car, which would be smashed up as it tried to go around and under the plough. The lump disappeared along the Panzer conveyor and down the face starting on its long journey to the surface. I smugly saluted it goodbye.

When it was completely out of sight I looked up to trim any loose coal that was still adhering to the roof, only to see everything moving. Unable to move a muscle in the next split second I watched, like a spectator, what was happening. Not only were the last pieces of loose roof coal starting to fall, but so was an area of roof about five yards long to the left of me and five yards to the right of me. I was right in the middle. The area on the move was about four yards wide for the full 10 yards length. The whole area was trembling. Small slabs of roof along with the coal fell, followed immediately by, what seemed like, the heavens. The whole of Glamorganshire seemed to be crashing down on me.

When the roof comes there's no warning, there's no noise but as it starts to crash over and around you the roar is deafening, even above the noise of the Panzer conveyor.

Everything happened in slow motion or appeared to, and as the roof fell towards the floor it took me with it. As the fall hit me I was swept downwards and backwards under the huge force. Hydraulic props and link bars were skittled out as if they weren't there. Crazily, I didn't let go of the jigger pick. I have heard of builders who have fallen off high ladders whilst carrying bricks and landed at the bottom still tightly holding onto the bricks. So it was with me and the jigger pick. We landed together as the roof crashed down all over me and around me. It seemed to come and come and just keep coming, rock after rock, slab after slab. And then the weight of the fall of roof staked the Panzer conveyer and all was silent. Just the last few stones from the dome shaped void, clattered on the heap above me.

I was buried with just my head showing. Releasing one arm I cleared what debris I could. Luckily my helmet had been knocked forwards and covered my face in the fall and taken the full force of the slabs of roof around my head.

My cap lamp was still alight and in that split second the reality of my situation overwhelmed me. Crumpled under the fall my frailty was so apparent, my youth had been no armour against the roof and Mother Nature had laughed at my insolence in the duel for coal and demonstrated that she was indeed no respecter of Howard G Awbery. My arrogant, self-acclaimed invincibility was a joke!

I lay there in silence, anxious that there would be another, even bigger fall, but there was absolutely nothing I could do about it, absolutely nothing! I tried in vain to move; nothing moved. The size of the fall had sent a blast of air down the face and in no time at all many cap lamps investigating the stoppage surrounded me. Soon, the only men in the whole world you want near you when you are staring out from under a fall of roof were comforting me. First, they made the place as safe as they could and then systematically started to work their way towards me clearing the fall as they neared me. It wasn't necessary for a discussion about a plan; every man knew what needed to be done.

I don't remember any pain at that time but I could sense the urgency in the voices around me.

Was I frightened? Of course I was frightened. Was I going to die? Not a chance because after working with these men for 11 weeks I had a confidence that somehow, everything would be alright. They worked quickly, glancing at the roof every few seconds looking for the tell-tale sign of another imminent fall. They were looking for that fine stream of dust falling from the cracks in the fragile, broken stone canopy above the void that is always the harbinger of the roof being on the move; slabs of rock under huge pressure grinding their way downwards to be suddenly released from their fingertip holds on other slabs of rocks. If you saw the fine dust then it would always, always, always be followed by another fall maybe even bigger that the last.

The Deputy tried to pull me out. He put his hands under my armpits as soon as enough space had been cleared and pulled. My shoulders were free but my body and legs were trapped. I remember screaming; the more he pulled the more I became aware of the searing pain in my left leg.

The Deputy uncovered the Tannoy and snapped an instruction to both ends of the face. In minutes more men were coming, each sweating with the difficulty of travelling quickly in the low conditions, wondering what they were coming to. There must have been about 15 men there by the time they had all arrived and without any discussion they surrounded the rock that was crushing my lower body and took the strain. Nothing…then you found out why he was the Deputy. He snarled and growled at the men to try again and this time with redoubled efforts; he retightened his grip on my shoulders. This time the huge slab was lifted just a couple of inches by the straining colliers, just long enough to pull me from under. I must have passed out at that stage for the next I knew I was further down the face having been dragged to a place of safety.

Free from the fall I lay on my back looking up at the safe roof. I don't know what went through my head at that time. I was just pleased to be under well supported roof once again. My head was cradled on the knees of the Deputy. I looked down at my legs. Both of my knees were in their correct position pointing upwards towards the roof. My right foot with its steel toecap also pointed upwards towards the roof, but my left foot and its boot flopped, Charlie Chaplin-like, to the side causing a red-hot poker of pain to shoot through my whole body. I contorted into the sitting position and grasped my left thigh to prevent any further movement, only to be gently but firmly eased onto my back again by concerned hands. Amazingly, my only injury was a crushed left leg and some bruising and grazes to the other. I am not embarrassed to say that tears welled up in my eyes when I looked back at the fall and it became apparent how lucky I had been.

I remember I said a little prayer.

Morphine was administered on the coalface and with such a racing pulse it wasn't long before its effect reached my leg. My feet and legs were professionally lashed together to form a natural split and I started the long journey out on the, all too familiar, stretcher. I had never been transported on a stretcher before or looked at the roof from this perspective but I decided, there and then, if ever I have to carry anyone else out of a pit again I'll be far more considerate than ever I'd been in the past.

People ask me if I felt as though I was going to die. Never once did the thought cross my mind. My absolute faith in those who came to rescue me superseded any such thoughts and my belief that they would get me out of the pit, the two long miles, was a given. I am proud to have worked with such men and my regret is I will never to be able to show them. One day I will go back to Ponterdulais and find those who remain or their sons or daughters and shake their hands.

***

There followed three months in Moriston Hospital, which surprisingly was one of the most hilarious periods of my life. I was in a hospital ward of just colliers; many from Brynlliw Colliery, but the rest came from far and wide across the coalfield. Their injuries were many and varied but what they had lost in limbs they made up for many times over in character. My crushed, left fibular and tibia were manipulated back into a reasonable shape and a plaster cast from my toes to my crotch installed with the stern words of the Ward Sister ringing in my ears 'and don't even think of asking to get off the bed for at least six weeks!' (a far cry from techniques adopted in this day and age).

Memories of some of the antics of the other patients still make me smile. One practice was to assist each other to make breakfast. It had become common practice for the nurses to boil an egg for each patient. Now, hospital eggs were battery eggs and had as much flavour as eating the box they came in. So it was agreed that we could cook our own eggs if a member of our family brought them in for us. Most of us had supermarket eggs, but one old collier had his own chickens and his wife brought in eggs that looked as big as duck eggs and had the most golden egg yolks. How did we establish whose egg was whose when they were all in the pan together? Well, the simple way was to write your own name in pencil on the shell, and then there could be no mistake.

The next day at visiting time my request changed from six eggs to six eggs and a rubber. When it was my turn to boil the eggs I rubbed out the old collier's name and substituted my own. His name was substituted for mine on my, much inferior, egg. Three weeks I managed to get away with it until he was being discharged and asked me how I did it. When I told him he roared with laughter, told me I'll go far, wished me well and I never saw him again.

Black humour was the order of the day. Men having lost a leg below the knee would raise up their stump for the doctor on their morning rounds to shake the knot at the end of the tubular bandage. Young nurses would be asked for bed socks by colliers who'd had one leg removed and when she had put one sock on and she couldn't find the other foot, she would either give the man a playful slap or run down the ward screaming.

Jokes would regularly be played on each other. The man in the next bed to an electrician we all called Grumpy decided he was fed up with his constant complaining and would give him something to complain about. He got up in the middle of the night to use his night bottle that was beside his bed. However, instead of getting out and using his own bottle, he deliberately got out of bed on the wrong side and used Grumpy's bottle. No problem there then. Not that is until Grumpy decided to get out of bed some time later and use his own bottle. As the already three quarters full bottle started to fill it soon became apparent to Grumpy what was about to happen. Squealing for a nurse at three in the morning as pee was splashing everywhere woke the whole ward who, when they realised, what had happened and to whom, were beside themselves laughing. It wouldn't have been half as funny if it had been with anyone else.

I was issued with crutches which were to be my travelling companions for the next six months and discharged from the hospital. I remember when my father came to collect me; we had to make a small detour on the way home to collect some doves that I had won in a game of cards from another patient. My father just shrugged his long-suffering shoulders and suggested we put them in the garage until the morning and I was to leave it to him to tell my mother. One year later I was registered as 15% disabled and given a lump sum of about £70 as I was no longer able to play football, go climbing, surfing, water-skiing or ball room dancing. (Thinking back, I'm slightly embarrassed now that I may have used a modicum of poetic licence when describing my hobbies to the awarding panel, especially the ball room dancing bit.) In 1964, £70 was a considerable sum of money, enough to put a huge deposit on a brand new Mini with my old Austin Cambridge as part exchange.

So at least one good thing came out of my experience.

Chapter 3 - Three National Strikes

Two shadowy figures pushing a wheelbarrow full of red-hot embers skulked from the brickworks across the 400 yards of no-man's land back to the colliery. They stopped only to lift the heavy, hot wheelbarrow over the main line rails. The time was 3.00 am and their coats and scarfs were secured as tightly as possible against the vicious December weather and their cap lamps switched off so as not to be seen.

The sleet had turned to snow and the wind tore across the open land, fanning the embers in the wheelbarrow with each gust of wind leaving a trail of sparks. For two weeks the weather had been deteriorating and sleet, rain and cold had been the order of every day. If ever there was a time for coal miners to be on strike, this was it.

Eventually, arriving at the shaft side, the wheelbarrow was carefully emptied into a fire brazier and more wood added.

Soon the shadowy pair had a blaze roaring that even this wild wind and snow could not extinguish. I was one of those shadowy figures and Joe Otterwell was the other. We were engineering trainees working at Pye Hill Colliery and this was the sister pit at Jacksdale called Pye Hill number 2.

Pye Hill number 2 was the downcast shaft that fresh air went down before it travelled on its long journey ventilating the pit to reach the upcast shaft at Pye Hill number 1 Colliery. Our mission was to ensure that if the temperature dropped below zero degrees then we were to light several large fires on the surface at the shaft side to warm the air going down the downcast shaft.

If we were unsuccessful then the water that found its way into the shaft, half way down, from the surrounding strata would freeze, closing the gullies that directed this water safely into the downpipes. When the gullies were frozen the water would still keep coming from the strata, but would then cascade over the frozen gullies and run down the shaft walls, forming huge sheets of ice that cloaked the shaft wall. When the warmer weather resumed that was the time for trouble. Slabs of ice sometimes 100ft long by 10ft' wide and up to two feet thick would suddenly fall, ripping out the shaft furnishings as the shards crashed to the bottom of the shaft. Icicles 20 yards long would suddenly break free and javelin-like, impale themselves into the decking at the pit bottom. No men were allowed to ride the shaft when there was ice of this magnitude present. If Pye Hill number

2 could not be ridden then it meant there was only one means of egress for either pit and all production would cease. The number of men allowed down would be reduced to nine.

There were no shaft heaters at Pye Hill number 2, so the age-old method of warming the air by open fires before it entered the shaft was adopted. The reason we were slinking over to the brickyard was because over the last two weeks it had rained and sleeted until everything was as damp and soggy as it could be. Try as we might we couldn't light a fire and what we did light wouldn't have warmed a sausage. Then we spotted the fires in the brickwork kilns. We hunted for a wheelbarrow, went over keeping a lookout for the brickwork's night watchman and helped ourselves. The snow soon covered our tell-tale tracks back to the colliery and once the fires were burning brightly we were able to relax in the knowledge that the shaft wouldn't freeze… bugger the bricks.

The situation of just Joe and me being there in the dead of night had come about by the National Union of Mineworkers calling an all-out strike. On 09/01/1972 the National Union of Mineworkers asked for a 43% increase in wages and was offered 7% by the Government. The offer was considered derisory and the NUM went on national strike for the first time since the 1926 general strike. A state of emergency was declared by the Government of the day and a three-day working week was imposed across the country to save electricity. However, on 28/02/1972

41

the miners accepted a compromise and became the highest paid workers in the UK.

During the strike essential work was allowed to keep each pit safe. As we were not seen as a threat, Joe and I were allowed to carry out such work. We were members of the Official's Union, NACODS (National Association of Colliery Overmen, Deputies and Shot firers).

Being top of the wages league was not to last for the miners and within one short year they had dropped to 18th place in the earnings league. At the same time the Arab/ Israeli war was pushing up the price of oil, a situation which the miners believed they could exploit. With the recent success of flexing their collective muscles fresh in their memories, the young bucks urged the Union for another showdown. On 09/02/1974 the miners came out again on a national strike; only the second time since the General Strike of 1926.

Again the government declared a state of emergency but this time to make the situation bite even harder in the UK, they started to switch off domestic power to every home. Believing the public had been critically inconvenienced by the miners and hence lost public support, the Government, headed by Ted Heath, promptly called for a general election and was soundly defeated. The miners not only won the strike but also won an additional long-running battle for compensation for pneumoconiosis victims.

There followed a relatively peaceful industrial relations time in the British coal mining industry.

It was to be 10 years (1984) before the Union would again flex its industrial muscle. With the threat of the closure of some 70 pits, the National Union of Mineworkers went on the rampage, picketing working pits and coking plants. Nervous that the NUM executive wouldn't obtain a full mandate for another national strike, they allowed each union area to decide itself. Only Nottinghamshire and parts of Derbyshire decided to continue working, being the most profitable pits with the best futures. At that time I was working at Bentinck Colliery as Deputy Manager under the best Manager I ever worked for, David Crisp. We split the duties between us and worked alternate weekends to carry out essential work.

By some twisted Union logic, even in the Nottinghamshire area, neither men nor officials who normally inspected the pit were allowed to work at weekends, leaving all the essential weekend work and inspections to be carried out by management. Work, like underground inspections or shaft inspections, meant members of the senior management team had to don shaft harnesses and ride on top of the cage to examine the shafts. As I had spent two years working in the shafts at Gedling Colliery, this was not an inconvenience to me but for those unfamiliar with shaft work it was the worst possible job on God's earth.

Those managers unfamiliar with this type of work would gingerly climb onto the top of the cage and cling to the bull-chains that secured the corners of the cage to the rope. There they stayed for the duration of the ride, often with their eyes shut tight! They gunshot flinched every time the signal plate was hit with a hammer, the signal to ascend or descend. However, there was always one of us competent so it was not of huge concern. Also, the shafts were examined by regular, experienced shaft teams throughout the week. Along with the examination of the headstocks, the examination of the downcast shaft was a bitterly cold task during the winter months, which encouraged me to feel more kindly disposed towards those men who requested warmer clothing when things did return to normal.

We formed two teams of management to cover the weekends. David Crisp, the Colliery Manager, took one team and I took the other. I felt that if we had to be there and undertake such duties, for what looked like becoming a very long haul, then my team needed a treat when all of the work was done. So, in my team we took it in turns to cook breakfast for the whole team every Sunday. There were probably 15 of us in my team.

The breakfasts started modestly enough, for instance just, 'a full cooked'. By 'a full cooked' I mean a full cooked for Desperate Dan i.e. 1/2lb sausages each, 1/2lb bacon each, three eggs each, three inches of black pudding each and so it went on. Oh, and not to forget a mountain of toast and preserves. Every Sunday the conference room table was set properly with flowers in the centre, napkins and place mats, glasses for fruit juice and proper coffee. However, it wasn't long before the more adventurous among us had tired of sausages, bacon and black pudding and moved on to more exotic fare.

Smoked salmon, croissants, patés and smoked haddock became the order of the day and when we tired of these we chose themed breakfasts from around the world. Menus would be in the language of the country and it was part of the fun to try to guess what we were going to have.

These breakfasts were a welcome departure from the routine of pit life during strike situations. They were harmless, neutral and everyone looked forward to a good fun Sunday extravaganza. Never was any work left undone and never was work shortened to accommodate the 'breakfast'. I learned from this small but fun experience the value of teams having occasions to look forward to. They were like a prize earned when the work was done. They welded my team into a cohesive, productive, high performing outfit.

There were bad times in the strikes and I never want my children to see what I saw especially during the 1984/5 strike. There were occasions when the NUM secretary from Bentinck Colliery, Neil Greatereaux, went on TV and declared that Nottinghamshire would not go on strike until a full national NUM ballot had been held. I winced each time it happened for the outcome was predictable. The next morning 3,000 Yorkshire men would descend upon Bentinck Colliery to 'discuss' the matter with him. This usually meant me being there at 3.00 am and liaising with the police and my men as to how the morning shift should confront the pickets. I witnessed in the early days up to 1,000 police in riot gear plus police horses and police dogs all preparing for war.

Police spotter squads watched from vantage points identifying the trouble makers in the picket lines and as soon as the news teams and TV camera teams had gone and my men had been escorted into work, then the police 'snatch teams' would move in. Few snatched pickets arrived at the mobile prison vans, out of view of the press, in one piece. I don't ever want to see such violence again on these shores, whoever is to blame.

There were some highlights during the strikes. One I recall was when Avonmouth police officers were camped at Bentinck Colliery for a week on a 'just in case mode'. To dispel the boredom they went down to the local video shop and rented say, 10 videos to pass away the hours of inactivity. Around 10.00 am the Chief Constable approached me to say their intelligence reports indicated a large number of pickets were on their way to Bentinck Colliery. His request was for me to hide the rented video player and videos. Astounded, I inquired if they thought the pickets would get inside the colliery offices, only to be told that the pickets were not the cause of his concern. His anxiety was caused because the Metropolitan Police were being sent as reinforcements. 'The Met', he explained, as all their propaganda stickers said, 'are magic' and had a reputation for being able to make anything disappear!!

By half way through the strike I had had my fill of the press displaying all miners as brick throwing louts. These were in the minority of even the most ardent pickets. I decided I would have my own campaign to redress the balance. I decided to have an exhibition of the craftsmanship of the men who worked at Bentinck Colliery. I put aside a small training room off the main conference room and put the word about.
As I have found in life, when I commit myself publically to anything Providence lends a hand and shortly, following my announcement of the exhibition, two of my men came to see me and asked if they could have their two weeks holiday and also a further

week's unpaid leave to walk from John-o-Groats to Land's End.

I agreed, as they expected, but before they had exited the office block I had come up with a plan and called them back into my office. Their extra week's leave was conditional, if they would walk, then we would arrange sponsorship for them and I would pay them the extra week. Of course they agreed.

Minutes later I was on the phone to an old colleague John Simmons, currently MD of 'On Communications in Oxford' but back then a South Nottinghamshire geologist, to see if he could arrange for Dr David Bellamy, the well-known conservationist and presenter, to host a short film advertising the walk. Two weeks later following a trip to Dr Bellamy's house in Durham, I had my film of a celebrity advertising the walk, encouraging sponsorship for funds for The Crown School (now called Fountain School) for children with learning difficulties in Nottingham.

Three weeks before the exhibition was about to open and contrary to my critics, the inquiries started to come in to see if certain things were eligible. Promises of exhibits came from wine makers, model makers, bow makers, wood carvers, pyrogrophers, embroiderers, stick makers, glass engravers, and painters. I was staggered, not only did we need to open the whole of the training centre; we had to open the whole of the conference room as well. There were wood carvers who asked if there would be security on the building, as the insurances of their carvings, up to £6,000 each, were not covered without security. A Deputy at the pit and a first class oil painter asked if he could sell his paintings and price tags of £2,000+ were added. Everyone sold.

This was a humbling point in my career.

What a terrible indictment on me!

Here I was, the Manager of 1,000 men, and I didn't know what skills and abilities I had under my nose. How could I manage these people if I didn't know what I had? I remember walking around this superb exhibition shaking my head at the lack of my knowledge. A truly humbling moment.

From that moment on I looked at every man who worked for me not as an employee, but as a person who I was fortunate to have working at my colliery. Each person came with special skills and abilities and it was my job to find out what those skills were and align their skills in a way that the colliery could best benefit.

The exhibition was a huge success. It redressed the negative TV and press coverage and a considerable sum of money was raised for the Fountain School. It also brought together the whole pit in a concerted effort to achieve.

And such a salutary lesson for me!

Chapter 4 - The Ghost

As Manager of Cotgrave Colliery in 1988 in the Nottingham area, the morning figures were on my desk as I arrived, as was my cup of tea.

My temper for the day was determined by that simple sheet of paper. A clue to its contents was set by whether the guy who made me tea in the mornings was still present in my office. If the figures were good, I would be met with a cheery, 'Well Gaffer, K1s did well yesterday.' Or, on the other hand, his absence was the harbinger of poor figures and to be well out of my sight line had historically proved the most painless option to him. I was met with his cheery greeting and sat down to examine the figures. Today there was nothing outstanding. Today's figures were just OK.

Each coalface is given a number which is preceded by a letter to donate the seam being worked, K represented the Blackshale seam, T represented the Tupton seam and W represented the Waterloo seam.

K 1s had achieved two cuts on night shift and the other faces had achieved adequate performances, which meant Cotgrave Colliery had achieved its budgeted tonnage for the day. This was an infrequent achievement but meant that the daily report into HQ should be less painless for me than normal. In fact, the other faces had produced sufficient for me to keep some tons in hand for a less productive day in the future and so the charade of deciding how many tons to declare to HQ preceded the morning dual.

Cotgrave Colliery had been sunk in 1960 and sported two Koepe winding towers, the most modern winding engines in Europe. The colliery was populated by approximately 1500 employees many of whom, along with their families, had relocated from the Northeast. The drive south had been precipitated by the closure of perfectly good and productive but underinvested pits in the Northeast. Cotgrave Colliery boasted an estate of 1,060 tied houses as an inducement for the Northumberland and Durham men to move south. Other incentives of cash and prospects were set out before the families. Here was another startling example of political ineptitude and short-termism.

Cotgrave Colliery closed in 2006, leaving the miners feeling completely abandoned by the Conservative government who initially had driven them from the North East coalfields, encouraged their support in Nottinghamshire with promises of a secure future throughout the 1984/5 miners' strike and then abandoned them during the following closure programme.

Preceding my telephone report to HQ came my morning management meeting and the tenor of the meeting was always dictated by the production results. Good tonnage and the meeting was good humoured, poor tonnage and look out! Blood and snot often covered the conference room walls. Poor tonnage and we entered a cockpit of engineers all defending their own corners; the Electrical Engineer bitterly complaining about the lack of co-operation from the Mechanical Engineer and the same in reverse. The daily combat was both pointed and scathing, the Electrical Engineer calling the fitters 'spanner lads', the Mechanical Engineer calling the electricians 'sparkeys' and both referring to the Mining Engineers as 'rock apes'. Refereeing was often the order of the day rather than chairing.

On this particular occasion the good-humoured morning management meeting was nearly over when the Deputy Manager, John Gospel, exclaimed, 'that he nearly forgot but there had been a stretcher case the previous night'. Now, a stretcher case should have been the first item on the agenda of the morning management meeting, such was the importance of health and safety. However, he went on to explain. A young lad of about 20 years of age had been working underground on his own, in a remote place, where one conveyor fed its river of coal from the coal face onto another conveyor on its way to the pit bottom. On his mid-shift round of inspections the District

Deputy had found the jibbering young lad in a faint. Having revived the nearly unconscious lad the Deputy asked for an explanation to be told by the young lad that he had seen a ghost.

Now remember where the lad was working. He was working on his own 600 yards below ground, two miles from the pit bottom. He would see a Deputy at the beginning of the shift, once in the middle of the shift and once at the end. The remote area where he worked would have been sparsely lit and 50 yards in both directions the roadway would have been in complete darkness. The morning management meeting of hardened coal-mining men pooh-poohed the idea of a ghost and several humorous suggestions for the incident were proposed; dreaming, sleeping, drinking and magic mushrooms just to mention a few.

John Gospel went on to say that the Deputy had been unable to help the lad to even stand, his legs having turned completely to jelly and the more he stayed at the scene the more agitated the lad became. Terrified, the lad explained in graphic detail the apparition. He explained the ghost was a miner about 5ft 6ins, who wore a Sinkers distinctive white jacket (Sinkers were men who only worked in the shaft and historically only wore white donkey jackets for some inexplicable reason). The ghost wore an old style, black, moulded cardboard helmet long since banned underground, tied his trousers below the knees with string called Yorks and walked straight through the wall leading to a blocked off old roadway not 10ft away from where the young lad worked.

The Deputy, himself a hardened mining man of many years' experience had been unnerved by the lucid description and the state of the lad. He immediately arranged for the young lad to be carried out of the pit on a stretcher and into the Medical Centre. Following a thorough examination he was taken home to rest. The lad was a good worker, had never had done anything like this in the past and was totally reliable… a mystery.

It was decided in the meeting to keep the incident as quiet as possible, true or false, for if the newspapers got hold of a story like this then who knew where it would lead? The day passed without incident with only the occasional reference to the previous night's casualty.

Our habit was to meet up as Colliery Manager and Deputy Manager at about 5.30 pm to discuss the events of the day and plan the rest of the week. John and I were having such a meeting. Suddenly, the phone rang. It was the telephone exchange, only manned up until 5.00pm by permanent staff who always filtered calls to me. A well-meaning security man put the call directly through to me. The call was from a woman who had asked for the Colliery Manager and before I could ask the nature of the call, the stand-in telephone exchange man had put her through.

Out of courtesy I let her continue. She explained that she and her husband had lived in Cotgrave village many years ago but now she lived in Devon. Her husband had worked at Cotgrave Colliery for several years but sadly had been killed in a pit accident. The previous evening he had appeared to her in Devon to warn her. She continued to explain that he had tried to tell her that something was about to happen at Cotgrave Colliery and the woman felt it her duty to warn somebody. (At this point I put the phone on speaker so that John would be able to listen).

Several times through the conversation she apologised saying that I might think her mad but pleaded with me to hear her out. She didn't know what was going to happen, she didn't know when it was going to happen, but she took the visit from her deceased husband very seriously. He had never visited her before and the experience completely unnerved her. She gave me her name and contact details and on request she furnished me with her deceased husband's name, saying he had died in a shaft accident… He had been a sinker.

How much credence does one put on the warnings of a woman some 200 miles away? Are mining folk susceptible to warnings from ghosts? Remember the poem, 'Don't go down the mine Daddy'. Is the power of St Barbara, the patron saint of miners, stronger than that of a ghost? Who knows, but the experience unsettled two fairly level-headed mining engineers. We decided to keep this part of the ghost mystery to ourselves. However, just in case, not that we had been affected by the experience you understand, we put in place a series of safety training practices for every person who was engaged in work around either of the two shafts.

The following morning every training record was examined and all of those men who were nearing the time to renew their certificates had their training brought forward. In a period of about three weeks we had the most trained and well documented, workforce of the whole of the mining industry.

In the background, some quiet investigations were taking place. Mr George Fletcher (Area Sinking and Tunnelling Engineer) was tentatively asked by me about the death of the sinker at Cotgrave Colliery. He revealed that a sinker of that name had indeed died in a shaft accident. He could describe him. He was about 5ft 6ins, wore a sinker's white jacket, never wore knee pads but tied his trousers below the knee with Yorks and insisted upon wearing his comfortable moulded, black, cardboard helmet long after they had been banned. These pieces of information became more and more uncomfortable as they unfolded. (The first part of the jigsaw.)

Various friends of my family who knew mediums, asked them in a semi light-hearted way to try to contact the unfortunate sinker, but to no avail. What they did all have in common though was the vision of orange flashing lights whenever they tried to communicate with him, but they couldn't interpret the meaning of the orange flashing lights.

***

Like all warnings, time dimmed the urgency of the warning from the ghost and so it was with John and I. That is, until Saturday evening about a week later when it was my weekend on call. At about 6.00pm I received a call from the pit to say that 'the UNOR system was acting up'.

Now the UNOR system is a clever system of thin tubes that run for miles throughout the pit. It is a system that takes remote samples of air from around the pit and pumps these out to the surface for the quality of the air to be analysed. What was the analysis looking for? It was looking for minute traces of carbon monoxide amongst other things. Why look for minute traces of carbon monoxide? Because carbon monoxide is one of the first indicators of an underground fire.

Underground fires fill miners with dread. Your choice when you smell smoke underground is to either walk towards the fire hoping it isn't too far away so you can pass the fire to get on the fresh air side of it or walk with the smoke until you reach fresh air. Both options carry risk. To this end every miner now carries a self-rescuer on their belt to get them to safety. Without a self-rescuer fires are deadly. Here were all the signs of a fire underground.

Cotgrave Colliery had been registered as a low-risk, spontaneous heating colliery. Nevertheless, as a new mine thankfully it had been installed with all the latest monitoring equipment. The joke was that with such a low calorific value the coal from Cotgrave Colliery (i.e. canol coal, which is very high in ash) would only just burn with a fire lighter tied to every lump! Therefore, whenever the UNOR system alarmed in the past nobody had taken it seriously.

Having just left a high-risk spontaneous combustion colliery and been involved with several very unpleasant spontaneous combustion fires, I was in no way prepared to listen to a complacent control room attendant who wanted a quiet Saturday night to watch TV.

I set up a full emergency procedure from that moment on and our family evening was abandoned. I left for the pit at about 7.00 pm on Saturday having rung an old colleague who was the Regional Chief Scientist, Mr Neville Wood. Mr Wood had accompanied me on many such incidents at my previous colliery, Bentinck. 120 parts per million of carbon monoxide in a return airway were enough to encourage him to leave his comfortable fireside, get changed and go down the pit with me to investigate, even on a Saturday night.

We discovered a spontaneous heating had started on an old coal face that had stopped turning coal some 12 months previously and, through lack of manpower, was still to be salvaged. As always seemed to be the case, the abandoned face and spontaneous heating was as far away from the pit bottom as it could be. Hand-held equipment helped to identify the inaccessible fire area and between us we made the decision to stop off the roads leading to the old face to eliminate its source of air. In so doing, I abandoned £10m of mining equipment. It was that or risk losing the pit at a cost of about £½ billion.

Now, to build the walls to stop all of the air getting to a face takes manpower, lots of manpower. At the pit on a Saturday night there was a maximum of 10 men, so I despatched the Deputy Manager to go to Cotgrave Miners' Welfare at what was now 10.00 pm to round up enough men to start the work.

Imagine the scene. Cotgrave Miners' Welfare was a thriving, purpose designed, workingman's club that was heaving with not a seat to be had anywhere after 7.00pm on any Friday, Saturday or Sunday night and this was no exception.

 The music was pumping; the cigarette smoke would have been working its way down from the roof towards the floor as the evening progressed. Some folk were dancing in the aisles. After nearly four hours of drinking nobody spoke quietly anymore and the quiet area near the bar was a joke! The main 'turn' of the night was in full song competing with the audience when, in from the back of the concert hall came the Deputy Manager in his pit clothes. Black as the ace of spades, lit flame lamp still swinging from his belt and cap lamp flashing on his helmet as he walked, he viewed the scene. Through the smoke and dancing couples he wove his way towards the front of the miners' welfare concert hall. Through the drink-laden rows of tables of men and women enjoying their Saturday night he peered searching out the men he needed.

Some men would look for overtime whenever it was available, but they were not always the ones you wanted and others didn't want to be spotted as it would spoil a good night at the club. Instructing/requesting men to return to the pit on a Saturday night would not make you Mr Popular. The conversations would have gone like this…

"Manager wants you back at the pit."

"But I've been drinking."

"Perhaps a couple of pints will help you to drive your fork lift truck faster!"

"What about my missus?"

"Can she drive a forklift truck?"

"No."

"Then she stays here. There's a lorry outside waiting to take you back to the pit and if you look sharp you'll be back here for the last pint!"

The Deputy Manager went up and down the rows of tables and when he couldn't find who he was looking for he went into the snug, then the billiard room and even into the toilets to find them.

The 'turn' eventually stopped singing as the buzz of interest got louder with more folks facing the back of the room than facing the front. When the Deputy Manager was satisfied he had enough of the right men he turned to the stage and said to the 'turn', "Sorry Luv, I'm all done," and promptly marched out of the club behind 30 or so men with his flame lamp still alight and swinging off his belt.

As the spontaneous heating took hold through the night the parts per million of carbon monoxide began to soar, it became apparent that men without breathing apparatus wouldn't be able to work. It became the job for the Mines Rescue Service teams. These were requested from every rescue station in the Midlands and duly arrived at about 4.00 am on Sunday in their distinctive yellow vans each with their... orange lights flashing. (Another piece of the jigsaw?)

By 5.00am I was approached by the Canteen Manageress who explained that with such an influx of men there was no food left in the canteen. Every canteen in the area had contributed to replenish the stock in the emergency and now there was nothing left, not a crumb. She was about to close.

One thing you never do in an emergency is to close the canteen so I despatched a weary Deputy Manager with the Canteen Manageress in a lorry to the local village supermarket, where they copied the name from the sign above the front door saying the owner had a licence to sell wines and spirits, found

63

out where he lived, knocked him up, took him back in the lorry and went through his supermarket like a dose of salts, clearing him out of everything edible from sausages to cereal, from frozen chips to crisps.

The canteen never shut!

I left the pit and went home for the first time in 36 hours.

After two days of the mines rescue teams working round the clock in breathing apparatus, the stoppings were on at each end of the face and I gave instructions to evacuate the pit. This was a one-off. I can't ever remember hearing of a pit being evacuated in my 30 years. It was time to sit and wait. It was a nerve-wracking time for me.

Everyone watched the graph of the remote monitoring station as it rose and rose. It was the first thing they did when they arrived. If the graph didn't return to normal then it could be assumed that the fire had caught hold and the whole pit was in jeopardy.

The pit was evacuated for three days until the graph reached its zenith, eventually starting its slow journey back to normality, meaning that the stoppings had excluded the fresh air that fuelled the fire. Only then was it deemed safe to re-enter and examine the site. Eventually, life returned to normal at Cotgrave Colliery.

It was 5.30 pm about a week later when I had another call from the deceased sinker's wife. This time I was pleased to take the call.

"He's been back to see me and said it's all over now and the pit's safe." declared the excited woman.

Coincidence or what? Do I believe in ghosts? Would I have responded so quickly without her warning ringing in my ears? Were my antennae on high alert to anything and everything? Who knows? The only thing I do know is if John and I had not responded as quickly as we did there could had been 1500 miners and their 4,500 dependants moderating their lifestyles and hunting for work in the Nottingham area the following week...

... or worse!

Chapter 5 - Retirement Functions

The late 80s were a time when life-long careers in coal mining came to an abrupt end. The industry halved in size year on year by the early retirement of admin staff, engineers, mineworkers and officials alike. About 500 men left Bentinck Colliery over the period and the pit was the poorer for it. We lost characters, we lost talent and we lost the soul of the pit.

As Colliery Manager I tried to interview every man who was leaving. Some had tears in their eyes at the thought of losing what, to them had been their family, their life. They put on a brave face and talked about 'the wife' and the long list of jobs she had lined up for them, like decorating and filling their time with a bit of gardening, but the future was bleak for such active men and we both knew it.

Some of these men I had the highest regard for. They were giants amongst their peers; men whose wealth of experience would be lost at a stroke. Here was a political travesty unfolding in front of me of such magnitude that my great, great grandchildren would end up paying for the short-sightedness of the politicians of the day. They will look back and ask of us: 'How, on an island that stands on coal have we ended up being held to ransom for fuel by the rest of the world?' The politicians of that era should hang their heads in shame.

The whole raping process of the industry got better or worse depending on how one viewed the charade. And what did they decide would be the selection criteria for men to be chosen to go (sorry, be made redundant)? Was it by contribution? No. Was it by a man's choice? No. Was it by experience? No. It was by age! Can you think of a more ludicrous selection method? More of the political nonsense we suffered in a rush to close down the British Coal industry.

As soon as a man reached 50 years of age he was effectively sacked. Many times I would be experiencing a major problem at the pit which could have been so easily rectified by these experienced men. Problems like a major fall of ground on a face where we suffered because of the lack of experience to master the problem quickly or, more importantly, prevent the fall occurring in the first place.

I recall seeing one of the men I referred to earlier, a man whose command of men and respect from his men I so envied, having completed all of 'the wife's' list of decorating and his bit of gardening', now following behind her in the supermarket with two bags of shopping. Such a sad sight and he was embarrassed when he saw me. I so desperately needed his capability and foresight and solution-based thinking back at the pit and he so desperately wanted to be back in the environment where he felt at home. The ridiculous situation had arisen where I was the most experienced man at the pit on major falls and I was the Colliery Manager.

However, as with all these barmy ideas from on high, my management team and I set out to make the most of the situation. We decided that some of the more senior management and officials would enjoy a leaving party. Now, a Bentinck Colliery leaving 'do' was not like any other 'dos' I have ever experienced.

The previous Colliery Manager, David Crisp, was moving on to another pit and I was to take over from him. His leaving 'do' was to be held in a large restaurant and about 100 of his Bentinck Colliery colleagues were present. The tables were set out in a U-shape and the presentations were made. I can't recall what we gave him but it would have been something tasteful as he was one of the most well respected managers Bentinck Colliery ever had.

The presentation over, it was up to me to conclude the proceedings. My speech went something like this…

"When David Crisp first came to Bentinck Colliery he relied very heavily on the knowledge of the Assistant Manager called Sid Straw to help him through his first few uncertain months. At his previous colliery, Calverton, when David Crisp first arrived there he relied heavily upon an Under Manager called … to help him through those first uncertain days." (I had researched and found out the correct name. In fact, I was able to go back to most of his previous pits and actually named the correct person in each case.) I concluded the speech with: "I have been right back and found out who helped you, David Crisp, on your very first day in your new chosen career in the coal mining industry. The very first day when you didn't even know the difference between inby and outby; the very first day when you needed a guide to show you around and help you through those first uncertain days. David Crisp meet... SPARKY." And we led a pit pony into the restaurant across the carpeted floor and up to the top table.

The pit pony was closely followed by the Admin Manager carrying a bucket and shovel, just in case.

This function set the scene for many such evenings to come.

The restaurant became accustomed to our retirement functions and welcomed up to 100 heavy drinking miners as their cash outweighed the inconvenience. Occasionally, there would be a function where wives would be invited. But these were rare. One such function was for the retiring Admin Manager. His name was Malcolm Winfield, a grandfatherly figure who had been at the pit forever. His outside work activity was as a Scout Master, a fact we framed his leaving 'do' around.

The meal and speeches over, all the guests were led out into another bar as, unknown to them, the restaurant was to be cleared and a full campsite set up. This consisted of tents, a mock lit-up fire and about 40 bales of straw assembled around the campfire for seats. When the guests returned to what they expected to be the original restaurant they were invited to sit on the bales of straw and we all sang Ging-Gang-Goolie and such other old scouting favourites. He had an evening never to forget and so did we.

The very experienced Safety Engineer, John Robinson's time to go eventually came around. Now John had an unpleasant attitude towards coloured people and was renowned for his views on the subject. He would rant on about job losses and housing so his evening became framed around this fact. His function was to be held in the same long-suffering restaurant.

He walked into the restaurant blind-folded; to be met by all the guests having blacked their faces and wearing white gloves. The whole group greeted him in the same poor Jamaican accent: "Halloooo der Joooohn."

The meal was served by the waitresses who, to give them credit, didn't even turn a hair, just lifted their eyes skywards and said 'it's just Bentinck's management team.'

He was presented with exactly what he had asked for, a 12-inch sculpture of a black penis. When he opened it he was baffled and asked what it was, to be told he had been given exactly what he had requested, 'A nice prick'

"No, no," he corrected, "I asked for an ice pick, not a nice prick!"

Later he was duly presented with his proper ice pick.

The two Under Managers had belly dancers and Morris dancers respectively and so it went on.

The numbers dwindled down to small functions and we met at the Boar's Head in Hucknall, Nottingham. When all were present we would decide on how the evening would run. One conversation at such a gathering I can recall as if it were yesterday. When it was decided to get a round of drinks at the beginning of the small gathering we usually threw £5 each into the kitty and when that was gone we would all throw in another. This time Sid Hutchinson, Bentinck

Colliery's Surface Superintendent, a huge man of stature, presence and character declared a change: "No kitty this time. Tonight it's, a round a-piece!" After a quick count up it was discovered there were 14 of us. And so the '14 Pint Club' was born and to this day we still meet. The retirement evenings were always boozy and fantastic fun. Generally, after about eight rounds, nobody could remember who had bought a round and who hadn't and nobody cared.

There are no longer 14 members of the '14 pint club', far from it, there are about four, the rest are either dead or if they came they wouldn't know where they were. We no longer have 14 pints we have about three halves of beer each otherwise it would give us so many problems throughout the night! But we still lay a place for Sid and toast absent friends.

Chapter 6 - Colin Bottomore's Wedding

Colin Bottomore had been the silver-headed President of the NUM at Bentinck Colliery for many years and continued, following the 1984 strike, to be President when part of the Union broke away from the NUM and established the UDM (The Union of Democratic Mineworkers). He was a fair man whose positive reputation was shared on both sides of the fence. He and I had seen Bentinck Colliery through some difficult times in the 1984 strike and its aftermath and he had become someone in whom I could confide.

When he sent out invitations to the last three Bentinck Colliery managers to join him and his wife at their wedding, each was happy to accept. It was a measure of the relationship each shared with him in their time. And so it was that three colliery managers attended Collin Bottomore's wedding to Maggie along with about 200 colleagues and friends.

The day was a complete success and the evening celebrations was in full swing when a distraught new Mrs Bottomore declared quietly to the group of managers' wives that on the drive to the wedding that day their car had decided it had been driven one mile too far and had shuddered to a stop in a cloud of black smoke. A consequence of this was the touring honeymoon they planned could no longer take place and their deposit at the various holiday centres was non-refundable. This had not been said to enlist sympathy but it was just the way it was. Maggie and

Colin resigned themselves to a honeymoon in Kirkby-in-Ashfield.

When I heard this, I decided to help but in the most secretive manner possible, for I had to be mindful of working with Colin in the future and he must not be seen by anyone to be beholden to me in any way. That way we could continue to work together as Manager and UDM Secretary without criticism from either quarter.

I decided I would loan him the car I used for work. It was an old, sturdy, Russian-built Lada. The car was totally reliable but not fashionable. However, it also had the distinct advantage of being better than anything he had at this moment in time. It would give me a good excuse to use my pride and joy at that time of an Aston Martin DB6. I pulled him quietly to one side and made the offer. He was very appreciative and agreed that it would be in both our interests to ensure the offer was kept to ourselves.

It felt good to be helping a friend and I was comfortable he would look after my solid but reliable car. The evening continued with much dancing and drinking. As the celebrations were coming to a close I chanced to overhear a delighted new Mrs Bottomore whispering to a group of wives consisting of the wife of the NACODS secretary, the wife of the COSA secretary and half a dozen wives of charge men and machine drivers: "Isn't it kind of the Manager to loan us his car to go on honeymoon. I'm thrilled, but please don't say anything to anyone. Colin wants to keep it a secret!"

***

Towards the end of the 1984 miners' strike a phantom negotiator started to make his presence felt between the newly forming UDM and the Government. Both sides called him the Silver Fox. Many secret meetings were held with the Silver Fox as the politicians saw this as a way to break up the NUM. From the other side of the fence, the miners who wanted to break away from the NUM needed reassurances from the Government of the day that their jobs would be safe and their futures were assured if indeed they did break away from the NUM and form the UDM. It was rumoured, at that time, that Colin Bottomore had direct access to the then Prime Minister, Margaret Thatcher's private line.

Several men claimed the name of the Silver Fox but Colin Bottomore was not one of those. He would not have wanted any sort of recognition save in the personal knowledge that he had been party to saving the jobs and livelihoods of his men and their families.
I came across Colin and his wife Maggie many years later whilst I was on holiday. He was the holder of a market stall in Devon and was selling women's knickers. Not wispy thin briefs but the big woolly ones worn by the sensible, the ugly or elderly. We had dinner together and after much reminiscing he confessed he had been offered recognition from the politicians of the day in the form of a CBE or OBE. As

I expected, he had courteously but immediately turned it down. Here was just one more crass example of the distance between the politicians of the day and working miners. The politicians had no comprehension that, as a highly principled man, it would be a complete anathema for him to accept an honour from a capitalist society whose injustices to his fellow man he had spent all his life fighting.

Chapter 7 - A Colliery Carol Service?

At Bentinck Colliery there were always celebrations just before Christmas. Most colliery offices were decorated and the gardener, whose name was Ziggy, usually dressed up as Father Christmas and walked down the offices giving out small boxes of Smarties to everyone. He did it off his own bat, paid for the sweets and it became the start to Christmas. However, if there was a breakdown and the engineers were too busy in a meeting when he called then he would be told to f*** off and shove his Christmas. Ziggy usually responded by throwing half a dozen emptied boxes of Smarties through the open door, wishing them all a very merry Christmas and moving on, undeterred, to folk who were more in the Christmas spirit. Bentinck Colliery was a lively place to be at Christmas time.

In the offices on the very last day before we broke up, it was customary for everyone to get together, have a fine turkey lunch prepared by the canteen staff and then leave work early. The management team were no exception. The canteen order was placed, the meal served by canteen staff in paper hats accompanied by carols; crackers were pulled and everyone left for a well-earned Christmas break.

Christmas was always a nervous time for me with everyone's minds looking forward to the holiday celebrations. Concentration sometimes lapsed and occasionally serious reportable underground accidents were the result. There seemed to be a direct correlation between holidays and accidents; occasionally fatal accidents.

I was always pleased for my whole colliery to get to Christmas, accident-free.

Not only did the management team and the offices have a Christmas lunch but so did every face team, (days, afternoons and nights) on each of the four faces. They gathered together at snap time on the last shift in the main gate (a roadway leading to the face) and had what was called a 'fuddle'. Now, face teams differed on what constituted a fuddle. Some teams brought a few biscuits, mince pies and a couple of boxes of Twiglets, but others went the whole hog. Some face teams organised the fuddle with more planning expertise than a £10m coalface installation.

Weeks before, each man was given a list of what he should bring. When snap time was declared everyone went into the main gate and set out their contribution to the fuddle. Brattice cloth would be spread out for a tablecloth (Brattice cloth was a thin plastic membrane used to direct the flow of air and seal doors). On the cloth would be ham off the bone, fresh bread, pickles, sandwiches, scotch eggs, cheeses, pork pies, game pies all followed by traditional mince pies and Christmas cake, a veritable feast. Occasionally, beer would be secreted into the pit to wash down the feast but it was frowned upon by all. A party would be had and piped carols would be played all around the pit from the surface on the Tannoy system; a good, harmless start to Christmas.

By this time I had been at Bentinck Colliery as Deputy Manager for about three years and decided we needed to do something extra this Christmas. Whenever I announced I had an idea the Management team would groan in unison. This time I decided we ought to have our own carol service.

You can imagine that this idea was not met with huge enthusiasm, as but a handful of men and their families attended church. The idea was met with derision from all quarters but I'd been there long enough that if I got an idea into my head, then they knew there was no stopping me.

There was an order to achieving this project.

First, find a church. Fortunately, St Wilfred's church stood about 500 yards up the road on the brow of a hill. When I told the Vicar of my plan, he was sceptical but delighted. The thought of a full church for any occasion would be an exciting novelty for him.

However, I made the mistake of asking him if there was anything we could do to enhance the church for the service. He thought for a while and then his eyes shone. I shuddered to think what was coming next. He asked if we could light up the outside of the church for Christmas. As it was on a hill with few streetlights I conceded to the request. The electrical engineer, Billy Whizz was dispatched and over the next few days an arrangement of second-hand arc lights were installed pointing up at the spire.

The lights were duly switched on one evening and St Wilfred's church came alive. The lights were adjusted and St Wilfred's lit up brighter than Southall Cathedral. Delighted electricians stood back admiring their work. They had transformed this dismal church into a beacon of light in the darkness, calling parishioners to worship.

Out of the vestry ran the Vicar, cassock flapping behind him, shouting, 'turn it off, turn it off'. He had seen the electricity meter whizzing round about to take off. 'The cost', he kept shouting, 'the cost. We can't afford to turn it on'.

I won't repeat Billy's comments when the Vicar suggested 'by-passing the electricity meter' or what Billy Whizz said to him following other suggestions, but it left us with a bit of a quandary. How could we help if he couldn't afford to switch it on? Three days later I was told by Billy that everything had been sorted and, after assurances that nothing illegal had been done, admired the church bathed in light for our carol service and for Christmas. Billy really had done an amazing job.

I left the pit about 18 months later and it wasn't until then that I found out what he had done. Apparently, Billy had run an armoured cable the 500 yards from the pit all the way up the hill to the church in a deep trench and powered the church lights from the pit. Nobody else knew.

As the pit is kept open for pumping reasons it is likely that St Wilfred's church is still, to this day, lit up by power from the old colliery. I would be delighted if this was the case and the church is still lit every Christmas.

***

The next tricky bit was to get a congregation into the church for the carol service. My plan was to engage the help of the unions of whom many members had not entered a church since their own Christening, if then. Using the same tried and tested routine as before I went around the unions saying that the NUM secretary was doing a Bible reading at the carol service and would the NACODS branch secretary also like to do one? The same reply followed as always: 'Well if he's doing it, then so I will'. Quickly back to the NUM secretary before they could talk to each other and adopt the same routine in reverse. 'Well if the NACODS secretary is doing it, so will I'. Three more unions to go and I had all my readers.

Five union secretaries and their families were never going to fill the church so it was off to the local school for a junior choir and to another school for a junior band. These children would bring their parents who, in the main, worked at the pit. Add in the St John Ambulance Brigade (who all needed new uniforms to be signed off by me), the colliery brass band (who were looking for a new place at the colliery to practice), the fishing club (whose pond was on my curtilage and the threat of filling it in if I didn't get support could always be relied upon to swell the ranks) the management team (for the Christmas day, rota hadn't yet been completed by me), and of course, not forgetting those who genuinely wanted to go to a carol service and I had my first full church.

Mince pies and tea from the canteen were served at the end of the service followed by the management team going en-masse to the nearest pub and I was pleased that a new Bentinck Colliery tradition had been born.

The next year the church was full to bursting with folk standing in all the aisles. Nobody had to be cajoled; it was a lovely service and a delightful start to Christmas for us all.

On quiet moments, even now, I smile to myself and wonder if St Wilfred's church outside lights are still powered from Bentinck Colliery?

Chapter 8 - A Strange Request

A mining engineer's life is never dull or predictable. Every day in our underground world Mother Nature presents us with new challenges. It could be explosive methane gas, inrushes of water, unexpected faults or falls of ground; she is predictable only in her unpredictability. But a Colliery Manager's life is further complicated by the vagaries of people. If Mother Nature seemed complex in the demands she levelled upon me, it was nothing compared with the challenges posed by people. In my 25 years so far in the Industry at that time I thought I had heard most things. How wrong I was.

And so it was that on one very ordinary day an appointment had been arranged for me to meet with the Headmaster of, what was then called, the Crown School (now The Fountain School). I made it my business to be out of the pit and showered ready for the meeting. Even to this day I still reserve a special spot for the Crown School. The reason for my affection for the school is simple; for some little time prior to my meeting with the Headmaster I had inherited a situation where the Unions and management were truculent to say the least, downright bloody awkward is probably more accurate.

The Crown School served the purpose of welding the warring factions of the Unions and the management of Bentinck Colliery into a cohesive, successful team. Rather than focus on each other I suggested they focus on the neutral objective of raising funds for children with learning and physical difficulties. The outcome had been a transformation of industrial relations and harmony. I owed the Crown School a great debt and any request from the Headmaster would be met with a favourable reply. However, nothing could have prepared me for the request that was to follow.

The Headmaster began his tale that left me speechless. In his school were two brothers who were plagued by a terminal skeletal deformity. They were bright kids who, despite all of the operations and hospitalisation, accepted their burdens with a dogged cheerful resignation.

The eldest was about 14 years old, and as he neared the end of his short life the Headmaster repeated a conversation between him and the lad. 'Is there anything, anything you have always wanted to do? It dosen't matter how bizzare just tell me what it is and we'll see if we can set it up for you.'

The lad thought for a while and said he had always wanted to go up in a helicopter. After some more deliberation he added: "And I'd love to meet Brian Clough, the manager of Nottingham Forrest Football Club."

Three weeks later a helicopter landed on the Forest ground on a Saturday afternoon just before kick-off. The delighted lad disembarked and was pushed in his wheelchair to watch Nottingham Forest play from the dugout, with his hero, Brian Clough.

Within weeks the lad passed away.

My emotions were a jumble and I struggled to retain my composure. I said a small prayer of thanks for my two fit and healthy children and would not even allow mysef to even consider having to try to deal with the loss of either.

The Headmaster continued whilst I gathered my thoughts. The time was closing in on the younger brother and a similar conversation had been held. The lad explained that there were members of his immediate family who had always worked down the pit. He had heard them recount story after story and was intrigued. He had always wondered what it would be like to go underground.

Already my mind was racing ahead and gathering films of life underground, both in bygone times and modern. A visit to a mock-up coal mine museum was possible and a trip around the surface of Bentinck Colliery could be arranged to see the engineering workshops and coal preparation plant.

I wasn't prepared for the next bit.

"Could you take him and his friend down the pit and see what it's like for themselves?"

A long silence followed.

Not a chance. Two wheelchairs being pushed along underground on the totally unsuitable underground roadway surfaces.

Two wheelchairs amongst all of the moving vehicles loaded with tons of supplies for the faces. A huge risk?

Two underage, disabled lads in wheelchairs in a pit?

Not a chance. The idea was preposterous, impossible, dangerous. The risks didn't bear thinking about.

I remember mumbling: "No problem."

The meeting closed and a happy Headmaster left to tell the lad he and his friend were going down the pit! Now came the hard part. Convincing my team that we were going to do it.

They lined up to tell me all of the reasons why this was a very bad idea. The Safety Engineer, the Under Manager, the engineers, the Admin Officer. I always ended arguments with either, 'I don't mind what you do but remember where this particular idea came from,' or, 'if you won't do it your sucessor will.' But like all of my ideas, once they knew I was serious they threw themselves into the idea with heart and soul. They were a great team.

One week later and two wheelchairs were delivered to the pit to be modified to suit Bentinck Colliery's underground rail guage. There was the barrage of derogatory comments from the exasperated fitters e.g. 'the manager's becoming a lazy b....... now he wants to be pushed around the pit,' but that was all part of the culture.

As the visit day approached there was no shortage of miners who wanted to be part of the proceedings...
The day arrived and the two lads were kitted out with boots, overalls, helmets, cap-lamps and self-rescuers. They both had smiles fom one side of their faces to the other.

They were wheeled onto the cage and the gate closed. Three rings and the cage started its slow descent down to a world below to realise the boy's dream. Underground they were pushed along the rail tracks for about half a mile to a training face. Unfortunately, the rail track only went to the end of the coal face and they were unable to get a feel of what a coal face was really like from there. Without hesitation, and with no instructions from me, the two boys were picked up out of their wheelchairs by the colliers who worked there and carried onto the face.

They were both carried right up to the shearer (the coal cutting machine) and allowed to drive the huge machine.

They lowered and re-set the hydraulic supports, they started and stopped the powerful chain conveyor and they drove the coal cutting machine.

Next, it was on to see a roadway heading machine and then out of the pit for a bath and tea with the men from the face and their day was complete.

So was ours.

The boys were profuse in their thanks but we hadn't done them a favour. That boy, his friend and their bravery had done us the favour of allowing us into their world for a few moments. I never found out what eventually happened to him or his friend, but sadly I can imagine.

For all of us involved in the visit, the day had been one of life's humbling moments.

And finally, I left the British coal mining industry in 1994 on a Friday and started Awbery Management Centre the following Monday. A thriving company delivering management development to other industries. Management I had, in the main, learned during my amazing time in the British Coal mining industry.